MILLBROOK ARTS LIBRARY

PLACES
IN ART

by Anthea Peppin

The Millbrook Press
Brookfield, Connecticut

Copyright © 1991 Merlion Publishing Ltd
First published in the United States in 1992 by
The Millbrook Press Inc.
2 Old New Milford Road
Brookfield, Connecticut 06804

Design: Paul Fielder
Series Editor: Charlotte Ryrie

Printed in Spain by Cronion SA

Library of Congress Cataloging-in-Publication Data

Peppin, Anthea
    Places in art / Anthea Peppin.
      p.   cm. – – (Millbrook arts library)
    Includes index.
    Summary: Examines the way various artists depict different places
in their works and describes how to use such techniques as
perspective, light, details, and color.
    ISBN 1-56294-172-0 (lib. bdg.)
    1. Painting – – Themes, motives – – Juvenile literature. 2. Environment
(Aesthetics) – – Juvenile literature.   [1. Art – – Technique. 2. Art
appreciation.]   I. Title.   II. Title: Places in art.   III. Series:
Peppin, Anthea. Millbrook arts library.
ND1146.P47 1992
750'.1'1 – – dc20   91-34978
                                                        CIP
                                                        AC

Cover artwork by Richard Berridge and Gwen and Shirley Tourret
(B L Kearley Ltd); photography by Mike Stannard.

Artwork on pages 8, 14–15, 17, 22–23, 24, 32, 33, 35 by Paul Fielder;
pages 13, 18, 30 by Mike Lacey; pages 7, 12, 27, 38 by Andrew
Midgeley and pages 11, 31, 36–37, 41 by Edward Russell.

Photographs on pages 8, 14–15, 17, 22–23, 24, 28–29, 32, 33, 35,
42–43 by Mike Stannard.

❧
CONTENTS

The artist's place

The place where artists work is particularly important if they are painting directly from life rather than from their imagination. Some artists have a special place, or studio, where they always work. Perhaps they need a lot of equipment close at hand. Other artists have only a few materials. They can move around easily and choose different places to work.

When you look at the paintings in the pages that follow, you may be able to tell which ones were painted in the country and which were painted in a town. You may also be able to guess which artists

worked inside and which preferred to work in the open air. Many of the artists who paint places took materials with them. They painted places as they saw them. Can you think which images would be easier to paint outside and which could best be painted in a studio?

A Japanese painter at work

The Japanese painter in this picture is kneeling on the floor to work. He is painting a landscape with a long brush. He is probably working from memory, since he doesn't have sketches to follow. He seems to be painting quickly.

The Japanese artist Ando Hiroshige painted *Artist at Work*.

The artist's brushes, paints, and water bowl are neatly arranged on the floor beside him. This artist could probably work wherever there is a flat surface to rest on. He does not seem to need a special room for his painting.

Painting in a studio

The picture on this page shows the Dutch artist Jan Vermeer painting in his studio. Vermeer has painted a picture of himself at work. Can you see what kind of equipment Vermeer used in his studio? There is a wooden stand called an easel that held the canvas the artist painted on. There is a stool so that the artist could sit at the right height for his canvas. The heavy curtain was probably pulled across a window when Vermeer wanted less daylight to fall on his subject.

Artists such as Vermeer always worked in a studio. They sometimes copied models, as in this painting, or worked from sketches made outside. Sometimes they painted from imagination. They carefully prepared their canvases for paint and put the colors onto the canvases in a particular order. Their pictures took a long time to paint — sometimes a year or more.

How do you paint?

Do you sit on the floor and paint quickly like the Japanese artist? Do you paint carefully at a table or an easel like Vermeer? Paint a picture to show the place where you paint.

The Painter in his Studio was painted by the Dutch artist Jan Vermeer.

Special places

Mount Fuji in Clear Weather was painted by the Japanese artist Katsushika Hokusai.

Some people love the sea. Others love the countryside. Your favorite place may be in the heart of a city. Mountains were special to the artists whose pictures you see here. The Japanese artist Katsushika Hokusai and the French artist Paul Cézanne both sketched and painted many views of a favorite mountain.

Mount Fuji

In Japan, all mountains are sacred. Mount Fuji is one of the most sacred.

Hokusai drew hundreds of pictures of the mountain. Sometimes Hokusai concentrated on drawing Mount Fuji itself. Sometimes he drew unexpected views, perhaps showing a glimpse of the mountain hidden by a boat or a wave.

In the picture above, Hokusai has painted a pattern of different shapes and colors to draw attention to the mountain itself. The solid red mass of the mountain catches the eye.

Shapes and colors

Paul Cézanne lived near Mont Sainte Victoire in southern France. He studied this mountain again and again, often from different viewpoints. He painted it in watercolor and in oil paints. He sketched it in pencil and charcoal. Like Hokusai, he included details such as farmhouses and people in some of his pictures of Mont Sainte Victoire. The picture on the right shows the mountain on its own.

Cézanne was fascinated by shapes and colors. He has painted the shadow on the mountain as a pattern of strong colors. He has used rich, dark grays and blues to make the shadows look as solid as the rocks.

This picture, *Mont Sainte Victoire*, was painted by the French artist Paul Cézanne.

Your favorite place

Choose a place that is special to you in some way. It might be your house, or a place where you like to play. Paint a bold, bright picture that really captures the feeling of this place.

Look carefully at the place you have chosen and make some quick pencil drawings. Draw strong, bold outlines of solid objects. Use short, broken lines for the things that seem less important. Make notes about the colors you see.

When you have made several drawings, go home and paint your picture. Copy the shapes from your sketches, and concentrate on strong colors rather than details.

What is perspective?

The picture on the right is by the Flemish artist Pieter Brueghel. It is so realistic that it could be a view through a window. How did Brueghel manage to do this? He used a technique called perspective. When distance is drawn accurately in a picture, the picture is in perspective.

Foreground

The part of the picture closest to you is called the foreground. You can see plenty of details in the foreground of this picture. The dogs' footprints in the snow are clear. You can even see the dead leaves on the bushes.

Middle ground

The central section of a picture is called the middle ground. Can you see women gathering sticks for firewood here?

Background

The most distant part of a picture is called the background. Here, you can just see another village across the fields.

This painting by the Flemish artist Pieter Brueghel is called *February* or *Hunters in the Snow*.

Perspective model

Make a perspective model from three pieces of stiff paper. Divide each piece of paper into three sections by ruling faint lines from left to right. On the first piece, draw the images you want in your foreground. On your second piece, draw the middle ground on the middle section of the paper. Draw everything smaller than in the foreground.

Then fill in your background on the top of the third piece of paper. Now carefully cut around the top edges of your foreground and middle ground pictures. Keeping the bottom edges of the paper lined up, glue the middle ground onto the background. Then glue the foreground onto this. Does your picture look realistic?

The vanishing point

Regatta on the Grand Canal is one of many paintings of Venice by the Italian artist Giovanni Antonio Canaletto.

You may have seen paintings in which all the lines seem to lead to a dot in the distance. This dot is called the vanishing point. The vanishing point is an important part of perspective.

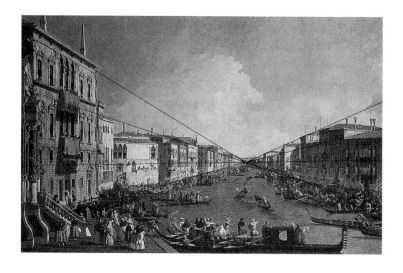

Straight lines

The Italian artist Giovanni Antonio Canaletto has used a kind of perspective known as linear perspective in this painting. This means perspective made with lines.

It is easy to tell where the vanishing point is in the picture. If you look at the diagram, you will see how the straight edges of the canal meet at one point in the distance. The lines formed by the buildings on each side of the canal end at the same point. Canaletto's picture is full of carefully planned detail. Every person or boat is drawn to fit in with the rules of size and perspective. He has used lines that meet at a vanishing point to create a feeling of space and distance.

A series of bridges

Can you find the vanishing point in this Japanese scene? The artist, Ando Hiroshige, has used the same method of linear perspective as Canaletto. He has also added other details to make us look toward the back of the picture. Look at the bridges in the picture. The bridge in the foreground is in the center of the painting, but the bridges in the distance are lower down. Your eye follows the bridges to the vanishing point in the background of the painting.

Experiment for yourself

Draw a simple picture using linear perspective. You need a ruler, paper, a pencil, and some colored crayons.

First decide where to mark your vanishing point. Is it to be high or low? Draw a very faint line across your paper, and put a dot on it to show your vanishing point. Using your ruler, draw two lines from this dot to the bottom corners of your paper. These lines will make a road or path. Are you going to have trees or buildings beside this road? Sketch them on your paper, remembering that the tops of the trees or buildings should follow an imaginary line that ends at your vanishing point.

You may need to practice before you get a good result. Take out your pencil and ruler and make lines across your picture whenever you want to check that you are getting things right. You can always erase the pencil lines later.

Kyo-Bashi Bridge and Take-Gashi comes from *One Hundred Views of Edo* by Ando Hiroshige.

Color and distance

During the 1600s, most European artists used linear perspective to create space and distance. Then they realized that objects could look different in color when they were farther away. If you look at a tree nearby, you can see every detail of its color. But a tree in the distance looks pale, and details of its color are less clear. It may seem hazy, as if covered with a light mist. European artists began to paint lighter colors for the background of their pictures to give a feeling of distance. This technique is known as aerial perspective.

Hazy, distant colors

The French artist Claude Lorraine worked in Italy and painted large numbers of detailed landscapes. Look at the way Lorraine uses aerial perspective in the painting on this page. Can you see how he changes the colors of distant objects? The foreground is full of dark greens, blacks, and blues. The hills and fields in the background are painted in light, hazy blues and yellows to show us how far away the hills are.

The French artist Claude Lorraine painted *Landscape with Psyche Outside the Palace of Cupid.*

Browns and blues

The Flemish artist Peter Paul Rubens also used color to create distance in the picture on this page. The foreground is painted in rich reds and browns, and the middle ground is dark green. The light, bright blue of the distance creates aerial perspective, which makes you concentrate on the details at the front of the painting. Can you see any birds in the bushes?

A color triangle

You can see how aerial perspective works by experimenting with bands of color. You will need paper and paints, a broad brush, and a piece of white paper. First draw a triangle. The bottom edge should be the full width of the paper. The point of the triangle should be in the center of the top of your paper.

Starting at the lower edge, paint a wide band of dark blue, red, or green. Mix a paler shade of the same color. Then paint another wide stripe above and slightly overlapping your first band, following your triangle shape. Keep mixing the paler shades of your first color and painting bands until you reach the top of the triangle.

Strength of color

You can use color triangles to guide you when you paint a landscape. Make a light pencil sketch before you begin to paint. Put some trees or bushes in the foreground, and remember to make all the details clear. Your background should be hazy. Now look at the colors in the paintings on these pages.

Next make a color triangle for each of the main colors you can see. When you mix a color for your landscape, first decide where in the picture you will be using that color. Then check the right color triangle to make sure you have not made your color too strong or too weak.

Landscape with Château de Steen was painted by the Flemish artist Peter Paul Rubens.

Pictures without perspective

A Tuscan Town was painted by the Italian artist Ambrogio Lorenzetti.

size as the ones at the front. The town is obviously on a steep hill, but there is little feeling that the sea in the background is on a different level.

Early Greek landscapes

We don't know the name of the Greek artist who painted the picture on the opposite page. But we know it was painted around 1500 BC. This huge painting covered one whole wall of a Greek house. Pictures such as these are called frescoes. Frescoes are painted onto the wet plaster of a wall. This fresco shows a landscape of hills, plants, and birds. Without knowing about the rules of perspective, the artist has tried to give a feeling of distance in his painting. He has drawn the birds in the sky small to make them seem far away.

This picture of an Italian town was painted in the 1400s. At that time, Italian artists often painted the same subjects. Paintings of stories from the Christian religion were common, and portraits were popular. But a bird's-eye view of a town was thought to be an unusual subject.

The painting looks unusual to us for a different reason. It was painted without perspective! The ground tilts upward so steeply that there is no room for the sky. The buildings at the back are the same

This is an ancient landscape fresco from Thera, in Greece.

Both sides of the painting are almost exactly the same. The two hills on each side of the central hill are mirror images of each other. The artist has deliberately painted a picture that is flat and balanced. This type of composition is called a symmetrical arrangement.

A balanced picture

You can have fun making symmetrical pictures. You need your brushes and paints and a sheet of white paper.

Fold the paper in half and open it out again so that it has a crease down the middle. Mix some thick paint. First, choose some strong greens and browns. On one side of the crease, paint one or two rows of trees. Work quickly so that your paint doesn't dry. Now fold the clean side of the paper over onto the painted side. Press down firmly. When you unfold the paper, the shapes you painted will have printed onto the other side.

A flat picture

Akbar Entering Surat is a Mogul miniature painting.

He did not worry about painting distance in a realistic way. The painting shows the emperor Akbar arriving at the outside gates of an Indian city.

There is so much activity in the painting that it is not immediately clear which figure is the emperor. Is he the man on the elephant at the front, or the man on the black horse? Akbar's black horse is surrounded by other people on horseback, on camels, and on foot. The people are all finely dressed in rich, brightly colored fabrics. Can you see the musicians dancing as they play?

No shadows

The artist has used rich red, gold, and orange colors to capture the heat of an Indian scene. The colors at the back of the picture are not lighter than those at the front. There are no shadows to make any figures in the picture look solid. The town walls are flat, as if they were cut out from cardboard. The artist is telling a story with his picture, rather than painting a realistic view.

Realistic flat pictures

During the 1700s, Dutch artists painted flat scenes on the inside of a box and viewers looked in through a peephole. These boxes were called perspective boxes. A well-made box could make a very realistic view. You can make a simple perspective box out of a small box with a lid. Ask an adult to help you cut down all four corners of the box.

When this Indian picture was painted, artists were respected people in India. They were employed by the emperors to record important events and stories in paintings. These artists painted flat pictures that didn't follow any of the rules of perspective.

Busy scenes

The Indian picture above is a Mogul miniature. The artist concentrated on the color and details of his scene.

Now you will have a flat shape. Leave one short side blank. On the other three sides paint a scene. Paint the base section of the box green. You could glue a twig in the center of the base to look like a tree. Then paint blue sky on the inside of the lid. You will need to cut a peephole in the middle of the unpainted end of your box. You will also need a hole in the lid so that light can shine into the box. Ask an adult to help you cut these holes. Join the sides of the box back together and put the lid on. Hold your box up to a light and look through the peephole.

Playing with perspective

Artists who were familiar with the rules of perspective sometimes played games with it. At first glance, the perspective of the two pictures on these pages seems to be normal. But look again!

False Perspective is an engraving by the English artist William Hogarth.

The fisherman

Look at the sign on the building in this picture. It appears to be behind the trees on the far hill! How could the woman leaning out of the window at the top of the picture light the pipe of the man on the distant hilltop? Can you work out the perspective of the tiled floor where the fisherman is standing? The English artist William Hogarth has thought carefully about the kind of tricks you can play with perspective. He has deliberately drawn some images in strange positions and others the wrong size.

An extraordinary building

Now let's look at the drawing by the Dutch artist Maurits Cornelius Escher on the opposite page. At first, it looks as if this is a detailed drawing of a house with many staircases. We think the picture is in perspective. But if you look at the picture carefully, you will realize that a building like this could not possibly exist.

Some of the figures going upstairs are upside down. Try turning the book around so that you can look at the picture from a different angle. You might expect the staircases to be the right way up now. But look again. Now another image will be upside down!

Draw a crazy cube

Complicated tricks with perspective such as the ones in the pictures on these pages are difficult to draw. The artists spent a long time working out the details in their drawings. You can draw a picture that is easier, but just as crazy! Try copying the "cube" below. Can you see how its perspective works?

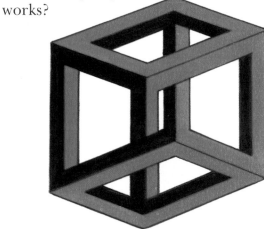

Going Upstairs is one of a series of complicated pictures by the Dutch artist Maurits Cornelius Escher.

Roman trick paintings

This is part of *The Fall of the Giants*, a mural by Giulio Romano.

A large mirror in the far corner of a dark room can make the room feel larger. The reflections in the mirror can look like the view into another room. The ancient Romans knew all about tricks like this, but they didn't use mirrors. Instead, they painted scenes on the walls of their rooms. These paintings were so realistic that people could imagine that they were not inside a house at all. Today, we call these trick paintings "trompe l'oeil," from the French words that mean "deceive the eye".

Jupiter and the giants

This photograph shows a small part of a huge painting that covered a whole room in a palace in Italy. The artist, Giulio Romano, painted the chief of the ancient Roman gods, Jupiter, on the ceiling of the room. Jupiter is surrounded by excited followers who are hurling thunderbolts at a group of giants below. Painted columns are tumbling onto the heads of the wild-eyed giants. Walking into this room must have been like walking into the battle!

The seashore in the city

This seashore scene was painted on a wall inside a Pompeiian house. Pompeii was a Roman town that was covered with ash when a volcano called Mount Vesuvius erupted more than 2,000 years ago. Beautiful paintings from houses there have been found, but most are incomplete or damaged in some way.

This scene was probably framed by a doorway. Can you imagine the feeling of seeing this pleasant watery view on a wall in your room? You might have felt as though you could have stepped through the door to wave to people on the opposite shore.

Can you see anything strange about the painting? The figures in the background are much larger than those in the foreground! The boat is as small as a toy. But the painting still gives us the calm feeling of a sunny day by the water.

A pretend window

Is there anywhere in your home where you would like to have another window? Perhaps you have a room with a small window, or a window with a gloomy view. You could brighten up the room with a large painted window.

Cut a piece of paper the size and shape of your ideal window. You may need to glue several pieces of paper together. Decide what you would most like to see from your window. Paint this view on your large piece of paper.

When your painting is dry, frame it with a frame the shape of a window. You can cut a cardboard frame and glue it onto your picture, or paint a frame over it. Then hang your picture on the wall. Does it look like a real window?

Sanctuary by the Sea is a wall mosaic from Pompeii, Italy.

Painted gardens

Nebamun's Garden comes from the tomb of Nebamun in Egypt.

The ancient Egyptians believed that you could carry your possessions with you when you died. People were buried with food, furniture, clothes — even jewels. The Egyptians also painted the walls of tombs with scenes from the dead person's life. The picture on this page is from the tomb of an Egyptian man named Nebamun. It shows the garden that he loved.

An ancient fishpond

In the middle of the garden there is a pond. Fish and ducks are swimming in the water, and lotus flowers are floating on the surface. On three sides of the pond, trees shade the water. We can clearly see what the garden was like, but it has been painted in a strange way. We see the pond from above, but we see the plants, ducks, and fish from the side. Some of the plants seem to be on their sides. Some are even upside down!

Faded colors

The Egyptians didn't think it was important to paint things as they actually saw them. They always showed things in the way that seemed most clear to them. This painting is more than 3,000 years old, so the colors have faded. But you can still make out traces of bright blues, greens, and yellows.

An emperor's wall

This scene was painted on a wall inside a Roman house. The painting is more than 2,000 years old. Life-size trees cover the whole wall. Many of these trees are covered with fruit. Painted birds fly in and out of the branches. Stories from the time tell us that the trees were so realistic that live birds used to fly up to the painting and try to peck the fruit with their beaks!

This garden was painted on the wall of the Villa Livia in ancient Rome.

An Egyptian water garden

Make a paper picture, or collage, in the style of the ancient Egyptian garden. You will need some old magazines, a large sheet of paper, some scissors, and a bottle of strong glue. First, make a small sketch to show what you want your finished collage to look like. Use this as a rough guide.

Now paint a pond in the center of your paper. From your magazines, choose some pictures of plants, fish, and birds. Make sure that the pictures have clear outlines and bright colors. Cut the pictures out and lay them on your backing sheet.

Look at the picture of Nebamun's garden again. Move your cutout images around, but be careful not to let any pieces overlap. When you are happy with your collage, glue the pictures down carefully.

Light and mood

Choose a particular scene from your neighborhood and look at it several times during one day. As the sun moves, see how the light changes. Different colors and shadows appear, altering the way the scene looks. Light also changes according to the time of year.

A group of French artists, called the Impressionists, were fascinated by light. One of the best known of the Impressionists was Claude Monet. When he was a young man, Monet stopped painting in a studio and started to paint all his pictures outside. He concentrated on painting the changes in color and shape caused by light at different times of the day. He wanted to catch the true effects of daylight on an object.

Monet's garden

One of Monet's favorite places was the water garden at his home in France. He painted many pictures showing a lilypond in the garden at different times. The bridge in this picture was white. But here, the shadows falling on the bridge make it appear green. This is because the light is reflected off the green trees and reeds behind the bridge. The whole picture is a beautiful mixture of greens and purples. Do you think it was painted on a sunny day?

A great cathedral

Monet also painted many pictures of the cathedral at Rouen, in France. Each painting shows the cathedral at a different time of day. In this painting, the colors seem to shine with reflected light. Most of the picture is painted in sunny yellow, but Monet has used darker colors to suggest the heavy doorways, towers, and windows of the cathedral. Even though the painting is full of light, we know that this is a strong building.

An impression of a building

One way of copying the Impressionist style is to paint on wet paper. Choose white paper to help the light shine through your picture. Take your painting materials outside on a sunny day, and find a building to paint.

Make a quick pencil sketch of the shape and main features of the building. Then make your paper wet by brushing or sponging water all over it. This will help your colors to flow over the paper. Paint the darker or shadowy parts of the building with darker colors first. Then paint the main part of the building with bright colors. Work fast, using small, quick brushstrokes.

Waterlilies was painted by the French artist Claude Monet.

The French artist Claude Monet painted *Rouen Cathedral at Sunset.*

Buildings

Gare Saint Lazare was painted by the French artist Claude Monet.

The best pictures of buildings don't just show us their shape and size. They make us feel as if we are walking around them, or even that we are inside the building itself.

A busy train station

Here we are in a busy, working train station. High over our heads is the tall iron and glass roof of the train depot. Billowing puffs of smoke and steam from the steam engines stand out as light patches against the dark roof. There is movement everywhere.

The painting is by the French artist Claude Monet. We have already looked at Monet's interest in light. Can you see the effect of the light streaming through the glass roof of the station onto the clouds of steam in this picture? Monet shows us how the shapes of people and engines stood out in the confusion of the smoke and noise of the station. He created the impression of activity by using patches of color instead of neat outlines. This is such a busy picture that we can almost smell the smoke and hear the bustle of the people!

A forgotten place

This picture has a different feeling. It shows an old ruined chapel where kings and queens of Scotland were once buried. There is no busy activity inside this building. Broken columns stand out against the night sky. They seem to stare down into the roofless building. Dark arches look like eyes watching the empty spaces. Moonlight streams in through the broken roof and windows, and there are patches of black shadow. This building looks lost and forgotten.

Clear details

The chapel has been carefully drawn. We can see every detail of the building as it looked when the picture was painted. Do you feel as if you are standing inside the chapel? The French artist who painted it, Louis Daguerre, wanted to paint in the most realistic way possible. Eventually, he gave up painting and became one of the first photographers.

Painting details

You painted a building in the Impressionist style for the activity on page 7.

Now try to paint the same building in a detailed style, like Daguerre's. Before you start painting, make an accurate pencil drawing to follow. Draw in as many details of the building as you can. When your sketch is complete, you can start to paint. Choose a fine-pointed brush so that you can paint in all the details on your sketch.

The French artist Louis Daguerre painted *Ruins of Holyrood Chapel.*

The sea

The French artist
Claude Lorraine
painted *A Seaport.*

The sea can be powerful and menacing. You may have seen a rough sea, or looked at pictures of shipwrecked boats and stormy waters. But the sea can also be calm and friendly.

What does the sea mean to you? Does it mean playing on sandy beaches? Do you think of boats and travel? Before railways, trucks, and airplanes were invented, the sea was the most important means of transportation. People and goods were taken from country to country by boat. Ships often sank and many people lost their lives.

Calm and secure

The sea does not look dangerous in this view of a port. The towering masts of the big sailing ships and the solid buildings seem calm and secure. Men and women chat on the shoreline as a slight breeze ruffles the water and the flags flutter on the boats.

Boulogne Sands was painted by the English artist Philip Wilson Steer.

On the beach

This scene shows a happy view of the sea. It is a painting of a warm, hazy day on the beach by the English artist Philip Wilson Steer. There is no feeling of permanence here. It is a picture of one afternoon — perhaps a holiday or a special outing. It may seem strange to you that the children are wearing so many clothes on the beach! The red and white striped objects are tents where people could change when they wanted to swim in the sea.

If you look at the dots and splashes of color in the painting, you can probably tell when it was painted. Look through this book and see if you can recognize the same style in any other paintings. Wilson Steer greatly admired Claude Monet and the other Impressionists, and so he copied their way of painting.

Painting the sea

You don't need to be beside the sea to paint it. You can paint from thoughts and ideas. Make a sketch of some things that make you think of the sea or the beach. It may be sailing boats or rocky pools, or shells like the ones on these pages. Paint your images with splashes of color and thick, bold brushstrokes.

Choosing a format

Before you start painting, you choose what shape you want your picture to be. Round, square, and rectangular shapes are probably the most common. We call a picture's shape its format. The format you choose often affects the way you paint your picture. These two pictures have different formats. The first is taller than it is wide. It suits a tall image, such as the standing figure. This format is called portrait, because artists often use it for portraits of people.

If you want to show images surrounding a figure, you might choose a wider format like the second one. This format is called landscape, because artists often choose it when they are painting landscapes.

Tall and high

The Chinese hanging scroll on this page uses a portrait format to show a landscape. The tiny people in the foreground contrast with the height of the distant mountains. The tall, narrow format of the picture helps the artist to show the mountains towering over the people below.

This Chinese scroll painting is called *Visiting a Friend in the Mountains*.

A wide scene

Now look at this painting by the Japanese artist Yashima Gakutei. There is a wide sweep of sea and sky, and the rays of the sun stretch out across the picture. The boats in the background seem very far away. The wide format helps the artist to capture a feeling of space and distance.

Experimenting with format

Look through this book and see how the artists have used format. Think about how the shape of a picture affects the way you feel about the subject. Then try using different formats for yourself. Take a piece of paper with a landscape format and sketch a town. You will have enough room to include buildings, trees, and cars. You could even show the surrounding countryside.

The Japanese artist Yashima Gakutei painted *Ships Entering Tempozan Harbour.*

Now paint a town on a piece of paper with a portrait format. You will have less space for buildings and countryside, but you may be able to put in some people in the foreground. Is this picture more crowded than your landscape format?

Let's look at composition

When you pick a bunch of flowers and arrange them in a bowl, you have to decide which colors and shapes will look most attractive together.

An artist preparing to paint a picture has to make the same decisions. The artist chooses the right arrangement of lines, colors, and shapes to match the feeling or meaning behind the picture. We call this arrangement composition.

Balance

Look at these sketches. In the first one, the tree is the same size as the house and the picture is balanced. The second sketch looks unbalanced because the tree is larger than the house. Artists often aim to create a balanced composition in their pictures because it is pleasing to the eye.

Shapes and lines

We can use a series of imaginary lines to help us work out how an artist arranges the shapes in a picture. We call these lines composition lines. Look at this painting by the Flemish artist Pieter Brueghel. Can you see the lines made by the trees, the men, and the houses on the left? The lines lead you to look toward the back of the picture. This helps Brueghel to tell a story in the picture.

The hunters in the foreground are walking wearily homeward. The people in the middle of the picture haven't seen them yet. But some of them are preparing for the return of the hunters by gathering wood to make the fires to cook a meal. Our eyes automatically follow the composition lines as we "read" the story the artist is telling us.

Making things look good

Make an attractive composition by pinning pictures to a bulletin board. If you don't have a board, you can use a square of thick cardboard.

Use pictures cut out from magazines, or a collection of your favorite postcards and photographs. Do you want to make a round composition like this one? Do you want to tell a story with your composition?

Look at the sizes, shapes, and colors of the pictures you have chosen. Think where you want spaces between them, and where they could overlap. You may have to move your pictures several times before you're satisfied with your composition and can pin the pictures into place.

February or *Hunters in the Snow* was painted by the Flemish artist Pieter Brueghel.

Unexpected views

Look at this picture by the French artist Edouard Manet. It is a close-up view of two people in a boat. But we can't see much of the boat and we can see only part of the woman. We don't know if the boat is on a river or on a lake. You might think Manet has chosen an unusual way of showing this scene. But the composition of Manet's painting shows us how it feels to be gliding on the water.

Boating was painted by the French artist Edouard Manet.

Cut-off figures

In Japan, artists had been painting unexpected views like Manet's for a long time. In this print from a woodcut by Kitagawa Utamaro, the head of one of the women is hidden behind a screen. Utamaro shows the scene exactly as he saw it, without worrying about showing the whole figure.

Rolling up the Blinds to Look at Plum Blossom was painted by the Japanese artist Kitagawa Utamaro.

Photography

Both Manet and Utamaro have chosen unusual compositions for their paintings. The images in both paintings look almost like photographs we might take today. Photographers can look at objects from unusual angles and capture them immediately on film. Manet was painting in the late 1800s, just as photography was becoming popular. He used composition like a photographer, to paint a passing moment in a realistic way.

Make a viewfinder

If you have a camera, you will know how to use the viewfinder to look at scenes from different angles. The viewfinder shows only one part of the scene in front of you. The rest is cut off from sight. The viewfinder inside the camera frames the scene you see.

You can make a simple viewfinder from thin cardboard. Measure four strips of cardboard, 4 inches (10 centimeters) long and ½ inch (1.5 centimeters) wide. Cut these out carefully and glue them together to make a square frame. Then look through some old magazines for pictures of houses or busy streets. Place your viewfinder over the pictures and look at them from different angles.

Do you think the pictures look more interesting if you hide parts of them? What impression do you get if you cut out all the sky? Does it look odd if you hide everybody's heads? Experiment until you find a view of a picture that looks interesting or amusing. Try to copy this view and then paint it.

Color and movement

A storm can completely change the way a place looks. A strong wind bends the trees and rain beats down. On a stormy day, even the most familiar place becomes exciting or frightening.

Landscape was painted by the French artist, Narcisse Diaz de la Peña.

Storm over a town

Have you ever seen a storm like the one shown in this painting by the French artist Narcisse Diaz de la Peña? The storm is everywhere. The angry sky is so realistic that it overshadows the town completely. Great patches of light flood down from the sky to light up parts of the hills and the town. Can you imagine yourself in the hills, hiding from the wind and the rain?

Agitated scenery

The style and the colors of the picture on the opposite page are completely different. But there is just as much movement. The wind bends the tall cypress trees and rustles the smaller bushes. The ripe, golden grain ripples in the wind. Curling clouds race across the sky.

The Dutch artist Vincent van Gogh painted many outdoor scenes like this one. His thick, fluid brushstrokes capture the movement of swirling skies and landscapes simply and successfully. His paintings in this style express a love of nature and a joy in life.

Create a stormy sky

You need some paint and a large sheet of white paper. You are going to paint with your fingers! Look at the first painting and think about a storm. As you think, practice moving your hand to imitate the movement of wind and rain in clouds or trees.

Wet your paper with a sponge dipped in water. This will help you to paint in flowing shapes and patterns.

Put your fingers into some dark-colored paint. Spread the paint in swirling movements across the wet paper, imagining the movement of clouds in a storm. Don't forget to let some white paper show through to add light to your picture.

Work quickly, and stop as soon as you are happy with the effect. If you overwork your picture, the final result will be too solid to suggest the movement of a storm.

The Dutch artist Vincent van Gogh painted *Wheat Field with Cypresses*.

Night light

Boulevard Montmartre at Night was painted by the French artist Camille Pissarro.

Have you ever studied the sky at night? On a clear night in the country the sky is vast, blue-black, and filled with thousands of stars. Some stars are just faint dots of light; others sparkle brightly. When the moon shines, its strange glow lights things up in surprisingly clear detail.

It is never completely dark at night in a town. The orange glow from electric lights means that you can't usually see the stars. But there are many other things to look at. The lights from moving cars cut through the darkness. Lighted windows turn buildings into patterns of light and dark.

Colors in the rain

You can't see the stars in the sky over this city. It is a painting of a rainy night in Paris, France, by the French artist Camille Pissarro. Light from shop windows, headlights, and street lights shines weakly through the thick rain. The lights are reflected in the wet street and sidewalk.

Pissarro's blurred brushstrokes give the impression of a view of the street through a wet pane of glass.

Fireworks

The night sky in this painting is lit up by fireworks. The American artist James Whistler has painted a firework display on the banks of the River Thames, England. Fireworks shoot up into the sky like twinkling stars. The bright light of the fireworks enables us to see clearly the masts of the boats and their reflections in the dark water.

Night through your window

You don't have to be outside to make a nighttime picture. Pissarro's picture of Paris was probably painted from a window in his studio.

You need a large piece of black paper and your paints. Use the silvery light of the moon or the golden glow of electric lights as the main focus of your picture. Paint directly on your paper with bright colors and blurred brushstrokes. Be brave about the way you paint — remember, you are just showing the outline of whatever images you can see in the dark!

The American artist James Whistler painted *Nocturne in Black and Gold.*

Modern cities

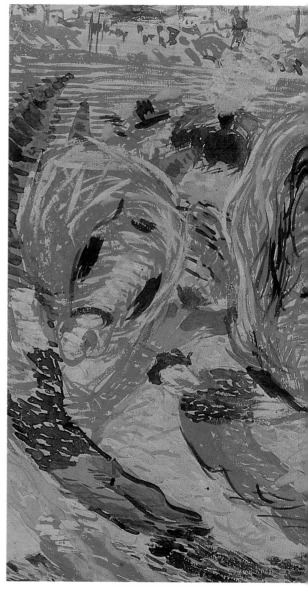

Cities are exciting places. People and cars rush through the streets. There is movement wherever you look! Buildings tower above you with tall, dramatic shapes.

Hustle and bustle

The Street Enters the House was painted by the Italian Futurist artist Umberto Boccioni.

Umberto Boccioni was an Italian artist who painted in the early 1900s. He was very aware that the modern world was constantly changing. He was excited by the power of machines. He used strong, bright colors and hard shapes to express the power of city life.

Both these pictures by Boccioni are full of color and energy. Can you see all the people hard at work in the painting on this page? As the woman leans over her balcony, she seems to become a part of the busy city outside her window. In the larger picture, Boccioni has used dramatic brushstrokes to show the power of horses moving through a city. How do the bold colors in these two paintings make you feel?

Breaking away from the past

Boccioni was the leader of a group of Italian artists called Futurists.

The Italian artist Umberto Boccioni painted *The City Rises*.

They wanted to break away from the traditions of Italian art. The Futurists captured the speed of modern life in their paintings.

Your own Futurist painting

Paint a picture of a street in the Futurist style. Sketch some ideas on paper before you start. Draw a street across the middle of the paper. Put some buildings in the background. Make them strong, square shapes. Then put more buildings along the edge of your street. They could be leaning over, or standing on top of one another to give a crowded feeling.

Your buildings can be all different shapes and sizes, but keep to straight lines and hard angles as you draw. If you show cars or buses in your picture, make them sharp and pointed to give an impression of speed. Remember to use bright, exciting colors when you paint.

How paint is made

Many of the pictures in this book were painted with oil paint. Others were painted with watercolors. Today, we can go to a store and buy different kinds of paints. Have you ever wondered how artists managed before modern paints were invented?

Early paint

Oil paint was not invented until the 1400s. Before this, most pictures were painted in tempera paint. Tempera paint was be made from a mixture of natural colors, or pigments, and egg yolk. Pictures using tempera paint were painted on a hard wooden surface. This wooden surface had to be specially prepared for painting. First it was covered with glue and then with several layers of liquid plaster, called gesso. This preparation made sure that the paint would stay on top of the wood instead of sinking in. If the wooden surface was not prepared carefully, the paint would crack. Look at some early paintings in

an art gallery. You will probably be able to see places where the tempera paint has cracked and bubbled.

Watercolors

Watercolors are paints made from pigments dissolved in water. They are much lighter than oil paints. Watercolors fade more easily than other types of paint. Watercolor pictures are painted on a kind of paper that lets the color sink in.

Oil paint

Oil paint is made by mixing the pigments with linseed oil and turpentine instead of egg yolk. Linseed oil comes from the crushed seeds of the flax plant. This is the same plant from which linen cloth is made. Turpentine comes from the sap of the pine tree. It is used to make the paint mixture thinner.

Oil paint does not flake and crack as easily as tempera paint. This means that it does not have to be painted on a hard surface. Instead, artists can paint on canvases. Canvases are made from fabric. The first canvases were made from linen cloth stretched across wooden frames.

Artists' biographies

A biography is the history of a person's life. These short biographies will help you to find out more about some of the artists mentioned in this book.

Umberto Boccioni (1882–1916)

The Italian artist Umberto Boccioni was fascinated by the modern world. As a young man, he painted realistic pictures. Later, he became the leader of a group of artists who believed that Italian art had been following the same traditions for too long. This group was called the Futurists. The name explained their interest in the future and their break from the past. Boccioni's paintings began to use bolder colors and brushstrokes, and his pictures became less realistic. Boccioni was killed when he fell from a horse at the age of 34.

Paul Cézanne (1839–1906)

As a young man the French artist Paul Cézanne was a member of the group of painters known as the Impressionists. Cézanne was an organized person, and he began to find the Impressionists' style too messy. Instead of copying an earlier style, Cézanne decided to start painting again as if he were the first painter in the world. He wanted to paint objects as firm, solid forms that were filled with light and color. Cézanne lived in the south of France and devoted his whole life to painting. His clever use of shape and color came to be greatly admired. The Spanish painter Pablo Picasso followed many of Cézanne's ideas. Picasso became the most famous painter of the 20th century.

Maurits Cornelius Escher (1898–1972)

The Dutchman Maurits Cornelius Escher specialized in extraordinary drawings. He created hundreds of very similar pictures that are interesting because they are all so complicated. His staircases and waterfalls seem to go up at the same time as they go down. At first glance, his buildings look realistic. But when you look closely, nothing is as it seems. Escher's drawings are based on his knowledge of mathematics and architecture.

Claude Lorraine (1600–1682)

Claude Lorraine was born in France, but worked mainly in Italy. He is sometimes known as Claude Gelée, or just as Claude. He first trained as a pastry cook, but he became the most famous landscape painter of the 1600s. All his paintings seem rather similar to us today. In the 1600s his ideas were considered completely new. Even when he was alive, his paintings were popular and very expensive. They were often copied by other artists, who tried to sell their imitations as real Claude paintings.

Claude Monet (1840–1926)
The first successful pictures drawn by the French artist Claude Monet were cartoons and funny sketches. These were instantly popular. But Monet's style changed as he became fascinated by painting light and nature. He became the leader of the group of painters known as the Impressionists. Monet's life was not easy. He was very poor, and his first wife was ill for many years. Many of his most beautiful paintings show places in the garden he created for himself and his wife. Monet began to go blind in 1908, but he continued to paint at home in his garden. His paintings became popular shortly before he died.

Italy. He was a talented and energetic painter. He could paint huge landscapes as well as portraits. Rubens was popular with the European rulers of the time, and was employed by them as a diplomat as well as a painter. He worked with various assistants and produced an enormous amount of work.

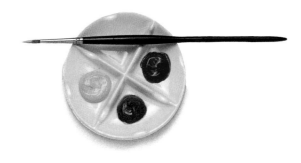

Peter Paul Rubens (1577–1640)
The Flemish painter Peter Paul Rubens was famous all over Europe during his lifetime. Born in Antwerp, he spent several years studying art in Spain and

INDEX

The publishers would like to thank the following for permission to reproduce these works of art:

A Tuscan Town (Veduta di una Città) by Ambrogio Lorenzetti; *The Fall of the Giants (Sala dei Gigante Parete eou Gigante e Colore); The Garden of the Villa Livia*; all by courtesy of Archivi Alinari, Florence, Italy; a Pompeiian mosaic, by courtesy of the Ancient Art & Architecture Collection, London, UK; *Going Upstairs*, a lithograph by Maurits Cornelius Escher, by courtesy of Museum Boymans van Beunigen, Rotterdam, Netherlands; *The Painter in his Studio* by Jan Vermeer, 1632-1675, in the Kunsthistorisches Museum, Vienna, Austria; *Mount Fuji in Clear Weather* by Katsushika Hokusai, 1760-1849, in the British Museum, London, UK; *Mont Sainte Victoire* by Paul Cézanne, 1839-1906, in the Buhrle Foundation, Zurich, Switzerland; *Hunters in the Snow - February* by Pieter Breughel the Elder, c.1515-69, in the Kunsthistorisches Museum, Vienna, Austria; *Regatta on the Grand Canal* by Giovanni Antonio Canaletto, 1697-1768, in Bowes Museum, Co. Durham, UK; *Landscape with Château de Steen* by Peter Paul Rubens, 1577-1640, in the National Gallery, London, UK; *Boating* by Edouard Manet, 1832-1883, in the Metropolitan Museum of Art, New York, USA; *Waterlilies* by Claude Monet, 1840-1926, in the National Gallery, London, UK; *Rouen Cathedral at Sunset* by Claude Monet, in the Pushkin Museum, Moscow, USSR; *Gare Saint Lazare* by Claude Monet, 1840-1926, in the Musée Orsay, Paris, France; *Wheat Field with Cypresses* by Vincent van Gogh, 1835-1890, in the National Gallery, London, UK; *Boulevard Montmartre at Night* by Camille Pissarro, 1831-1903, in the National Gallery, London, UK; *Nocturne in Black and Gold* by James Abbott McNeill Whistler, 1834-1903, in the Tate Gallery, London, UK; *The Street Enters the House* by Umberto Boccioni, 1882-1916, in the Niedersachsische Landesmuseum, Hanover, Germany; *The City Rises* by Umberto Boccioni, in the Collection Jesi, Milan, Italy; all by courtesy of the Bridgeman Art Library, London, UK; *Artist at Work* by Ando Hiroshige; *Kyo-Bashi Bridge and Take-Gashi* by Ando Hiroshige; *False Perspective* by William Hogarth; *Nebamun's Garden*; all by courtesy of the Trustees of the British Museum, London, UK; *Landscape* by Diaz de la Peña, by courtesy of the Fitzwilliam Museum, Cambridge, UK; *Landscape with Psyche outside the Palace of Cupid* by Claude Lorraine; *A Seaport* by Claude Lorraine; both by courtesy of the Trustees, the National Gallery, London, UK; *Boulogne Sands* by Philip Wilson Steer, by courtesy of the Tate Gallery, London, UK; *Akbar Entering Surat*; *Ships Entering Tempozan Harbor* by Yashima Gakutei; *Visiting a Friend in the Mountains*; *Rolling up the Blinds to Look at Plum Blossom* by Kitagawa Utamaro; all by courtesy of the Board of Trustees of the Victoria & Albert Museum, London, UK; *Ruins of Holyrood Chapel* by Louis Daguerre, by courtesy of the Walker Art Gallery, Liverpool, UK.

The publishers would like to give special thanks to staff at the Victoria & Albert Museum, London, and to Floyd Beckford and his colleagues at the British Museum, London.